Google Sheets for Beginners

A Quick and Step-by-Step Guide to Learn Google Sheets Fundamentals, Formulas, Functions, Macros, Management, and Visualization of Data

Harold A. Stokes

ISBN-13: 9798321681114

DEDICATION

To every one of my readers!

TABLE OF CONTENT

Introduction

Welcome to the world of Google Sheets, where numbers meet organization and collaboration thrives. Whether you're a student keeping track of assignments, a small business owner managing finances, or simply someone looking to organize information efficiently, Google Sheets has you covered.

At first glance, Google Sheets may seem like just another spreadsheet tool, but it's much more than that. It's a dynamic platform that empowers users to create, edit, and analyze data in real-time, all within a user-friendly interface.

The beauty of Google Sheets lies in its accessibility. No need to install software or purchase expensive licenses—just log in with your Google account, and you're ready to start creating and sharing spreadsheets with ease.

One of the most powerful features of Google Sheets is its collaboration capabilities. Gone are the days of emailing spreadsheet files back and forth or dealing with conflicting versions. With Google Sheets, multiple users can work on the same document simultaneously, making collaboration seamless and efficient.

But Google Sheets isn't just about collaboration—it's also about customization. From formatting options to formula functions, Google Sheets offers a wide range of tools to help you tailor your spreadsheets to your specific needs. Whether you're applying conditional formatting to highlight important data or using pivot tables to analyze trends, the possibilities are endless.

Of course, getting started with Google Sheets can feel overwhelming at first, but fear not. With a little practice and experimentation, you'll soon find yourself navigating the ins and outs of this powerful tool with confidence.

In the coming paragraphs, we'll explore the basics of Google Sheets, from creating your first spreadsheet to performing simple calculations and beyond. By the end of this guide, you'll have the skills and knowledge you need to harness the full potential of Google Sheets and take your data management to the next level.

So, without further ado, let's dive in and discover what Google Sheets has to offer. Whether you're a beginner or a seasoned spreadsheet user, there's always something new to learn and explore in the world of Google Sheets.

Chapter 1: Getting Started

1.1 Setting Up a Google Account

To get started with Google Sheets, you'll first need to have a Google account. These accounts are free, and the sign-up process is straightforward. To set up your Google account, you'll be required to provide some basic information, such as your name, location, and birth date. Once you've completed this process, your Google account will not only grant you access to Google Sheets but also automatically create a Google+ profile and a Gmail email address for you. It's a simple and efficient way to open the door to the world of Google Sheets and its collaborative features.

If you possess a Gmail address, the good news is you've got a Google account ready to roll. No need to go through the hassle of creating a new account; you can effortlessly log in to Google Drive using the same credentials as your Gmail.

Here's how to set up a Google account:

- Visit www.google.com. Look for and click on the sign-in button located in the upper-right area of the page.
- Choose the option to create an account.
- You'll be presented with a sign-up form. Simply follow the instructions and fill in the necessary details.
- Now, input your phone number. You will receive a verification code through a text from Google, and you'll use that to wrap up the signup.
- Type in the verification code sent from Google into the space provided and hit Verify.
- You will see a personal information page. Stick to the instructions and fill in the necessary details, covering your gender and birth date.
- Take a moment to glance over Google's privacy policy and terms of service, then hit the I agree button.
- Voilà! Your account is good to go.

Note: When using any online-based service, it's crucial to select a robust password—essentially, one that's hard for others to figure out.

1.2 Essential Google Sheets Terminology: What You Need to Know

Let's start by getting familiar with some key terms you should be aware of when working with Google Sheets:

1.2.1 Cell

A cell acts like a tiny box or compartment within a spreadsheet. It's where you place your data—numbers, text, or formulas—so you can organize and work with information. Each cell has its own unique address, defined by a column letter and a row number, making it easy to locate and manipulate data as needed.

1.2.2 Range

A range in Google Sheets refers to a group or collection of cells that are selected together. It's like highlighting a specific area within your spreadsheet where you want to perform actions, such as calculations or formatting changes. Ranges can be small or large, depending on the number of cells you choose. They're handy for organizing and manipulating data effectively, allowing you to work with multiple cells at once.

1.2.3 Row

In Google Sheets, a row is like a horizontal line that spans from left to right across your spreadsheet. It's where you lay out information side by side, whether it's names, values, or any other data. Each row is assigned a number, starting from 1 and increasing as you move down. Think of it as a neat way to organize your information horizontally, making it easy to read and comprehend.

1.2.4 Column

A column in Google Sheets is like a vertical pillar of information. Think of it as a neat stack of data running from top to bottom in your spreadsheet. Each column is labeled with a letter, making it easy to organize and locate your information. Whether you're dealing with numbers, text, or formulas, columns provide a structured way to arrange and manage your data. So, the next time you're working in Google Sheets, just remember: columns are your vertical buddies, holding your data in a tidy, organized fashion.

1.2.5 Worksheet

A worksheet, also known as a sheet, refers to the named collections of columns and rows constituting your spreadsheet. A single spreadsheet can house numerous sheets, allowing for organized data management.

1.2.6 Spreadsheet

This is the complete file holding all your worksheets together.

1.3 Creating Your First Spreadsheet

To kick off your spreadsheet journey on Google Sheets, you have four options to start a new one:

Method One

Click on the colorful "+" icon on the Google Sheets dashboard.

Method Two

Proceed to the Google Drive dashboard, click the colorful New button, choose Google Sheets, and click on Blank spreadsheet.

Method Three

Launch your Google Sheets spreadsheet, go to File, click on New, and select Spreadsheet from the menu.

Method Four

Simply enter "sheets.new" into your web browser.

This action will generate a new empty spreadsheet. You can also opt for a pre-made Google Sheets template, but for now, beginning with a blank spreadsheet is recommended.

1.4 Importing Data into Google Sheets

Bringing a file to Google Sheets is a straightforward process. You can import it right into the current spreadsheet, start a fresh one, or substitute a sheet (like a tab) with the imported data.

The files you will usually bring in are XLS and XLSX (Microsoft Excel files) or CSV (comma-separated values). To bring a file from outside your Google Drive, simply head to File, select Import, and click Upload.

Personally, I like to bring in the data onto a fresh sheet each time to keep my existing data separate from the newly imported one. Another option is that if you've got a Google Sheet (or a file like XLS, CSV, etc.) stored in your Google Drive, you are allowed to import it straight into the spreadsheet using the same method—just find it in your Drive within the import window.

1.5 Diving Deeper into Google Sheets

Google Sheets is an online spreadsheet tool where you can store and arrange various types of information, similar to Microsoft Excel. Google Sheets includes the most essential features needed for everyday spreadsheet tasks. It simplifies the process of creating and editing spreadsheets, whether they're basic or intricate.

Spreadsheets aren't just for number crunching or data analysis. They're versatile tools that can help with everyday tasks like creating invoices, garden planning, budgeting, and more. With spreadsheets, you can organize information effectively for various purposes.

Essentially, Google Sheets offers you the ability to arrange, modify, and examine various data types through spreadsheets. Here, you'll explore the diverse applications of spreadsheets and how to maneuver within the Google Sheets interface. Additionally, you'll grasp the fundamental techniques for handling cells and their contents, like selecting cells, inputting content, and copying and pasting cells.

1.6 Creating a New Spreadsheet

To start a new Google spreadsheet:

- Open your Google Drive and select "New."
- A drop-down menu will appear; choose "Google Sheets" from the listed options.
- A new Google Sheets spreadsheet will open in a new browser tab.
- To give your Google Sheets spreadsheet a name, find and click on "Untitled spreadsheet" at the top area of your page. Then, input the desired name for your spreadsheet and hit the Enter key.
- Your Google Sheets spreadsheet will now be renamed accordingly.
- Whenever you want to view or make changes to your spreadsheet, simply go back to your Google Drive, where it's automatically saved.

You might observe that there isn't a save button. That's because Google Drive employs autosave, which systematically saves your files instantly as you make changes to them.

1.7 Navigating the Google Sheets Interface

To work with and edit your Google Sheets spreadsheets, it's essential to get acquainted with the Google Sheets interface.

1.7.1 Understanding the Fundamentals of Cells

In any spreadsheet, you'll find numerous rectangles known as cells. A cell is formed where a column and a row intersect. Rows are labeled with numbers (1, 2, and 3), and columns are labeled with letters (A, B, and C).

Every cell in a spreadsheet has its own unique name, known as a cell address, which is determined by its column and row. For instance, if a cell intersects column E and row 8, its cell address is E8. When a cell is selected, you'll notice that its row and column headings become darker.

You can choose several cells simultaneously, forming what's called a cell range. Instead of using a single cell address, you identify a cell range by stating the cell addresses of the first and last cells, separated by a colon. For instance, a cell range covering cells C1, C2, C3, C4, and C5 would be denoted as C1:C5.

1.7.2 Working with Cell Contents

Every piece of information you input into your Google Sheets spreadsheet gets stored in a cell. These cells are versatile and can hold various types of content, such as text, functions, formulas, and formatting.

Here are the types of content you'll come across in cells:

1.7.2.1 Text

Cells can hold various kinds of text, including dates, numbers, and letters.

1.7.2.2 Functions and Formulas

Cells can hold functions and formulas that are used in the calculation of cell values. For instance, when you use SUM(D3:D9), it calculates the value of each cell within the range D3:D9, and you can see the total displayed in cell D10.

1.7.2.3 Formatting Attributes

Cells can also hold formatting attributes that alter how numbers, letters, and dates are shown. For instance, percentages might display as 20% or 0.20. You can even adjust the background color of a cell.

1.7.3 Selecting Cells

Before you can enter or make changes to the cell content, you must select the cell.

- To select a cell, simply click on it.
- Once selected, you'll notice a blue box surrounding the cell.

Alternatively, you can use the arrow keys on the keyboard to select cells.

1.7.4 Selecting a Cell Range

When you need to select a broader set of cells, or a cell range, here's how:

- Click and hold the mouse button, then drag it across the cells you would like to choose until they are all highlighted.
- Let go of the mouse button to confirm your selection of the appropriate cell range.

1.7.5 Inserting Cell Contents

Here's how to insert content into a cell:

- Choose the cell where you want to insert the content.
- Enter the content directly into the selected cell and hit Enter on your keyboard. The content will show up both in the formula bar and in the selected cell. You can also enter and make changes to content directly from the formula bar.

1.7.6 Deleting Cell Contents

Here's how to remove cell content:

- Choose the cell you would like to remove.
- Hit the Backspace or Delete key on your keyboard. This action will erase the contents of the cell.

1.7.7 Copying and Pasting Cells

Copying and pasting cells is a simple process. You can easily duplicate content already entered in your Google Sheets spreadsheet and paste it into other cells.

- Choose the cells you intend to copy.

- To copy the selected cells, proceed to your keyboard and use Command+C for Mac users or Ctrl+C for Windows users.
- Now, choose the cell(s) where you would like to paste the copied cells. You'll notice a highlighted box around the cells you've copied.
- To paste the copied cells, proceed to your keyboard and hit Command+V for Mac users and Ctrl+V for Windows users.

1.7.8 Cutting and Pasting Cells

To move content between cells in a spreadsheet, you can use the cut-and-paste function. Unlike copying and pasting, which simply makes a copy of a cell's content, cutting and pasting actually relocates the content from one cell to another.

Here's how to cut cells in your spreadsheet:

- Choose the cells you wish to cut.
- Hit Command+X for Mac or Ctrl+X for Windows on your keyboard. This action will cut the cells, but their content will stay in place until you paste them elsewhere.
- Choose the cell(s) where you would like to paste the content.

- To paste the cells, use Command+V for Mac or Ctrl+V for Windows on your keyboard.

If you need to copy and paste specific portions of a cell's content, the Paste Special option comes in handy. Navigate to the toolbar menu, click on Edit, then hover over Paste Special. From the drop-down menu, choose the specific paste option that suits your needs.

1.7.9 Dragging and Dropping Cells

Instead of using cut and paste, you have the option to drag and drop cells to relocate their contents.

Here's how to move a cell to a different location:

- Choose the cell you want to move, then hover your mouse over one of the blue box's outer edges. You'll see the cursor change into a hand symbol.
- Click on the cell and drag it to where you want it to be placed.
- Let go of the mouse button to drop the cell into its new position.

1.7.10 Using the Fill Handle

If you need to copy a cell's content to multiple other cells in the spreadsheet, the fill handle can help. Instead of manually copying and pasting into every cell, which can be time-wasting, use the fill handle to swiftly duplicate content from a cell to other cells in the same column or row.

Here's how to utilize the fill handle:

- Pick the cell you wish to work with. You'll notice a small square, called the fill handle, appearing in the cell's lower-right edge.
- Move your mouse pointer over the fill handle. You'll see the cursor turn into a black cross.
- Click and hold the fill handle, then drag it over the cells you would like to fill. You'll see a dotted black line on every side of the selected cells.
- Let go of the mouse button to fill the cells you have selected.

1.7.11 Continuing a Series with the Fill Handle

You can use the fill handle to extend a series in your spreadsheet. When your data follows a sequence, like letters (A, B, C) or months (January, February, March), the fill handle can predict the next items in the series. For instance, the fill handle can be used to extend a series of dates in a column.

Chapter 2: Working with Formulas and Functions in Google Sheets

2.1 An Introduction to Formulas and Functions

In Google Sheets, a function is a pre-set formula that calculates values based on specific inputs in a specific sequence. Google Sheets offers various common functions like minimum, maximum, count, average, and sum, which help quickly analyze a range of cells. To use functions accurately, it's important to understand the components of a function and how to set up arguments to compute values and cell references.

2.2 Understanding the Distinction Between Functions and Formulas

It's common to get mixed up between formula and function in Google Sheets. A formula is something you create using constants, cell references, and operators to perform personalized calculations or manipulate data. On the other hand, a function is a pre-set operation in Google Sheets designed for specific tasks and calculations, making common jobs easier with a defined purpose and syntax.

2.3 The Components of a Function

Just like when you input a formula, the sequence in which you enter a function matters. Every function has a set order, known as syntax, which you must follow for the function to compute correctly. The fundamental syntax for creating a formula with a function involves adding an equals sign (=), the function name (like SUM for finding the sum), and an argument. Arguments hold the data you want the formula to compute, like a range of cell references.

2.4 Understanding How Arguments Work in Functions

Arguments, which can be either single cells or ranges, need to be enclosed in parentheses. The number of arguments you include depends on the syntax specified for the function.

For instance, in the function =AVERAGE(E1:E9), it calculates the average of values within the cell range E1:E9. This particular function has just one argument.

When dealing with more than one argument, you need to separate them with a comma. For instance, in the function =SUM(D1:D3, F1:F2, H1), it adds up the values from all the cells listed in the three arguments provided.

2.5 Common Google Sheets Functions

In Google Sheets, there's a range of functions at your disposal. Here are some of the most frequently used ones:

2.5.1 SUM

This function calculates the total of each value within the specified cells.

2.5.2 COUNT

The count function tallies up the number of cells containing numerical data within the specified argument.

It's handy for a swift count of items in a given range of cells.

2.5.3 AVERAGE

The average function figures out the average of all values within the specified cells. It adds up the cell values and then divides that sum by the number of cells in the provided argument.

2.5.4 MIN

The min function finds the smallest value among the cells listed in the given argument.

2.5.5 MAX

The max function identifies the highest value among the cells listed in the given argument.

2.6 How to Create a Function

To use the Functions button to create a function:

The Functions button systematically computes results for a cell range. The answer will be shown in the cell beneath the range.

For the steps below, let's say we've got a range of numbers from A3 through A14 in your Google Sheets spreadsheet.

- Pick the cell range you would like to use in your argument. For instance, in our case, we'll choose A3:A14.
- Click on the Functions button. From the drop-down menu that appears, pick the function you desire. In this example, let's choose SUM.
- You'll notice the function appearing in the cell just underneath the ones you selected.
- Hit Enter on your keyboard, and the function will compute. You will see the result displayed in the cell.

2.6.1 Manually Creating a Google Sheets Function

If you're familiar with the function name, you can simply type it. For instance, let's say we have a list of sales amounts for various items from F3 through F9 in your Google Sheets spreadsheet. We'll use the AVERAGE function to find the average amount sold for the products.

- Pick the cell where you want the answer. In this case, let's choose F10.
- Start by typing the equals sign (=), then enter the function name you want to use. You are allowed to

choose the function from the suggested list that appears under the cell while typing. For example, let's enter =AVERAGE.

- When you're manually typing a function in Google Sheets, a window pops up showing the specific arguments the function requires. This window will show up once you type the first parenthesis and remain visible as you input the arguments.
- Insert the range of cells for the argument within parentheses. In this instance, we will enter (F3:F9). This formula sums up the values in cells F3 to F9 and then divides that sum by the total number of values in the cell range.
- Hit Enter on the keyboard to display the answer.

It's important to keep in mind that Google Sheets may not always alert you if there's an error in your function. Therefore, it's essential for you to review every function you use carefully.

2.7 Accessing the Google Sheets Function List

For those familiar with spreadsheets and looking to enhance their Google Sheets skills, the Google Sheets function list serves as a valuable resource. This compilation includes numerous functions, ranging from financial functions to data analysis and statistical functions.

If you've used the Function Library in Microsoft Excel, you'll discover that Google Sheets offers a similar array of functions in its function list.

- To open the function list, simply click on the Functions button and choose "More functions..." from the options.

This action will open the Google Sheets function list in a new tab in your browser.

2.8 Mathematical Formulas and Arithmetic Operators

In Google Sheets, you can perform calculations with numerical data. This section will guide you through creating basic formulas for addition, subtraction, multiplication, and division. Additionally, you'll learn how to use cell references in your formulas.

2.8.1 Formulas

Google Sheets offers a helpful function for managing numerical data effortlessly. Through formulas, you can perform basic arithmetic operations like addition, subtraction, multiplication, and division. This feature simplifies handling calculations, especially those involving one mathematical operation.

Usually, you'll use a cell's address in a formula, which is known as using a cell reference. This approach offers the benefit of automatic recalculation when a referenced cell's value changes. Employing cell references ensures the accuracy of the values in your formulas.

2.8.2 Arithmetic Operators

In Google Sheets, you'll find common operators for your formulas, such as:

- Plus (+) for addition
- Minus (-) for subtraction
- Asterisk (*) for multiplication
- Forward slash (/) for division, and
- Caret (^) for exponents.

Every formula in Google Sheets must start with an equals sign (=). This signifies that the content of the cell is a formula and represents the calculated value.

2.8.3 Making the Most of Cell References

When you include a cell address in a formula, you're using what's called a cell reference. Utilizing cell references in formulas is handy because it allows you to modify the numerical values in the cells without needing to write a new formula each time.

You can craft a range of basic formulas in Google Sheets by blending cell references with an arithmetic operator. Moreover, formulas have the flexibility to incorporate both numerical values and cell references, enabling diverse calculations.

2.8.4 How to Create Formulas

We'll make use of cell references and a simple formula to perform a straightforward calculation.

Creating a formula is a simple process. Follow these simple steps:

- Pick the cell where you want the calculated result to appear.
- Begin by typing the equals sign (=).

- Enter the address of the cell you would like to refer to first in the formula. You'll notice a dotted border around the referenced cell.
- Insert the operator you intend to use. For instance, input the addition sign (+).
- Input the address of the second cell you wish to reference in the formula.
- Hit Enter on the keyboard. Google Sheets will compute the formula, and the result will be shown.

To observe how the formula updates, try altering the value in any of the cells. The formula will instantly reflect the new value without requiring any manual adjustment.

It's important to note that Google Sheets may not always notify you if there's an error in your formula. Therefore, it's your responsibility to review and verify all your formulas for accuracy.

2.8.5 Point and Click Formula Creation Method

Instead of manually typing cell addresses, you can simply click on the cells you would like to use in the formula.

- Choose the cell where you want the calculated result to appear.

- Begin your formula by typing the equals sign (=).
- Select the cell you wish to include first in your formula. Its address will automatically appear in the formula.
- Input the mathematical operator you intend to use in your formula. For instance, you can enter the subtraction sign (-) for subtraction.
- Now, select the cell you wish to include second in your formula. Its address will also be added to the formula.
- After selecting the cell, simply hit Enter on the keyboard. The formula will then be computed, and the resulting value will be displayed in the designated cell.

2.8.6 Modifying a Formula

There are instances when you'll want to adjust an already existing formula. For instance, if you mistakenly typed the wrong cell address in your formula, you'll need to correct it.

If you need to change a formula:

- Double-click on the cell that holds the formula you would like to make changes to. This action will reveal the formula within the cell.

- Proceed to make the necessary adjustments to the formula. For instance, you can substitute a cell reference with another.

Once you've made the changes, simply hit Enter on the keyboard. This action triggers the formula to recalculate, and you'll see the updated value in the designated cell.

2.9 Introduction to Logical Functions

Google Sheets features logical functions that help you carry out operations and decide outcomes depending on certain conditions. These functions assess expressions or data and yield either true or false outcomes. They prove handy for tasks like data filtering, conditional calculations, and data analysis depending on particular criteria. In this section, we'll delve into some frequently used Google Sheets logical functions, offering examples to illustrate how they work.

2.9.1 AND Function

The AND function in Google Sheets assesses various conditions and provides a true outcome only when all specified conditions are met; otherwise, it yields a false result.

Here's a simple example: if you want to confirm whether both cells B1 and C1 have values greater than 10, you can apply the formula "=AND(B1>10, C1>10)." This formula will yield true only if both conditions are satisfied; otherwise, it will yield false.

2.9.2 IF Function

The IF function in Google Sheets stands out as a highly adaptable logical function. It enables users to carry out conditional tests or calculations depending on spelled-out conditions.

Example:

Suppose you want to determine if a value in cell E8 is greater than 20 and deliver a particular outcome based on the condition. In that case, you can make use of the formula below: "=IF(E8>20, "Value is greater than 20", "Value is less than or equal to 20")".

2.9.3 NOT Function

The NOT function is pretty straightforward. It takes one condition and does the opposite. So, if the condition is true, "NOT" makes it false. If it's false, "NOT" turns it true.

Here's an example to understand the NOT function:

If you want to see if the value in cell B3 is not equal to 5, you can use the formula "=NOT(B3=5)". If B3 doesn't equal 5, it will return true; otherwise, it will return false.

2.9.4 OR Function

The OR function checks several conditions and gives a true result if at least one condition is true; if none are true, it says "false."

Let's take an example: if you want to see whether either cell D1 or E1 has a value greater than 20, you should apply this formula: "=OR(D1>20, E1>20)". If one of these conditions holds true, it will return "true"; otherwise, it will return "false."

2.9.5 Examples from Everyday Life Using Logical Functions

Let's take a scenario where you have a Google Sheets document with student scores:

- Apply the IF function to allocate grades according to the scores. For instance, if the value in cell A2 surpasses or equals 90, designate "A"; if it falls between 80 and 89, designate "B," and so forth.

- Employ the AND function to verify whether a student's score exceeds 80 and attendance is over 90%. If both criteria are satisfied, label the student as a "high flyer."
- Utilize the OR function to verify if a student's score exceeds 70 or if they've finished an additional-credit assignment. If either condition is true, designate the student as "pass."

Utilizing logical functions within Google Sheets enables you to automate the grading process, pinpoint standout students, and assess pass/fail status depending on predefined conditions.

2.10 Google Sheets Comparison Operators

Comparison operators evaluate pairs of values, determining if they are equal, unequal, or if one holds a greater or equal value compared to the other.

Comparison operators operate on various types of values, including text, date, and time, as well as numeric values.

The comparison operator assesses whether the value on its left side matches, exceeds, or falls short compared to the value on its right side, resulting in either TRUE or FALSE.

<left-side value> (comparison operator) <right-side value> = TRUE or FALSE

Comparison operators yield either TRUE or FALSE, indicating whether a condition is met or not. This outcome guides whether a cell, column, or row requires a particular transformation.

2.10.1 Different Comparison Operator Types

Google Sheets offers six comparison operators for various operations. These operators include:

- Equal to "="
- Not Equal to "<>"
- Less than "<"
- Greater than ">"
- Less than or Equal to "<="
- Greater than or Equal to ">="

Now, let's delve deeper into the function of each of these comparison operators:

2.10.1.1 Equal to "="

This operator evaluates whether the value on the left-hand side is equal to the value on the right-hand side.

To carry out the 'equal to' operation, use the syntax:

$$=(value1 = value2)$$

Here, value1 and value2 represent the two values under comparison. These values can be Boolean values, date or time values, strings, text, numbers, or references to cells holding any of these types of values.

2.10.1.2 Not Equal to "<>"

The "not equal to" operator evaluates whether the value on the left-hand side is not equal to the value on the right-hand side.

To perform the 'Not Equal to' operation, you use the syntax:

=(value1 <> value2)

Value1 and value2 are the two values you are comparing, which can include Boolean values, date or time values, strings, text, numbers, or references to cells holding any of these types of values.

2.10.1.3 Less than "<"

The "less than" operator examines whether the value on the left-hand side is less than the value on the right-hand side.

To conduct the 'less than' operation, you use the following syntax:

=(value1 < value2)

Here, value1 and value2 represent the two values under comparison.

2.10.1.4 Greater than ">"

The "greater than" operator assesses whether the value on the left-hand side is greater than the value on the right-hand side.

To execute the 'greater than' operation, utilize the following syntax:

=(value1 > value2)

Here, value1 and value2 represent the two values under comparison.

2.10.1.5 Less than or Equal to "<="

The "less than or equal to" operator evaluates whether the value on the left-hand side is less than or equal to the value on the right-hand side.

The 'less than or equal to' operation is written as:

=(value1 <= value2)

In this syntax, value1 and value2 represent the two values under comparison.

2.10.1.6 Greater than or Equal to ">="

The "greater than or equal to" operator evaluates whether the value on the left-hand side is greater than or equal to the value on the right-hand side.

The 'greater than or equal to' operation is represented by the syntax:

=(value1 >= value2)

In this syntax, value1 and value2 denote the two values undergoing comparison.

2.11 Working with Google Sheets Text Functions

Let me introduce you to some fundamental text formulas in Google Sheets, along with examples. Whether you're a business owner, marketer, data analyst, or simply someone seeking insights from data, mastering basic text transformations in Google Sheets is essential. These skills are handy for swift analysis and data cleaning.

These text functions fall into four main categories, which include text capitalization, extraction, transformation, and meta function.

2.11.1 Text Capitalization

In real-world situations, obtaining clean data is not common, particularly when it originates from user inputs, and especially challenging if it's from a free text field. Text capitalization serves as a valuable method for standardizing string values in spreadsheets.

2.11.1.1 UPPER Function

The UPPER function is employed to transform every text character into uppercase.

Here's the syntax for the UPPER function in Google Sheets:

=UPPER(text)

For instance, if you have the text "hello" in cell A1, using =UPPER(A1) would result in "HELLO".

2.11.1.2 LOWER Function

The LOWER function converts text into lowercase letters.

Here's the syntax for the LOWER function in Google Sheets:

=LOWER(text)

For instance, if you have the text "HELLO" in cell A1, using =LOWER(A1) would result in "hello."

2.11.1.3 PROPER Function

The PROPER formula enhances readability by capitalizing only the first letter of each word in a string while converting the rest to lowercase. This approach adds a refined appearance and professional touch, making it suitable for management dashboards or reports.

Here's the syntax for the PROPER function in Google Sheets:

=PROPER(text)

For example, if you have the text "hello world" in cell A1, using =PROPER(A1) would result in "Hello World."

2.11.2 Text Extraction

The text extraction functions are handy for extracting text or characters from specific positions within Google Sheets cells. You'll likely find yourself using these functions frequently, especially when dealing with the task of standardizing inconsistent date formats.

2.11.2.1 LEFT Function

The LEFT function is handy for extracting characters from the leftmost position within a text string.

Here's the syntax for the LEFT function in Google Sheets:

=LEFT(text, [num_chars])

In the syntax, "text" represents the cell containing the text string, and "[num_chars]" is the number of characters you want to extract (optional, defaults to 1 if omitted).

For example, if you have the text "Google Sheets" in cell A2, using =LEFT(A2, 4) would result in "Goog." It extracts the first four characters from the left side of the text string.

2.11.2.2 MID Function

The MID function is a bit less direct than the LEFT/RIGHT formulas, but essentially, you specify the starting position of the character you want and then indicate how many characters you'd like to retrieve. After that, like magic, it works its charm!

Here's the syntax for the MID function in Google Sheets:

=MID(text, start, num_chars)

The MID function allows you to extract a specific number of characters from a text string, starting at a defined position. In the syntax, "text" represents the cell containing the text string, "start" is the position from which to start extracting characters, and "num_chars" is the number of characters to extract.

For example, if you have the text "Hello, World!" in cell A1, using =MID(A1, 7, 5) would result in ", Wor". It starts extracting characters from the 7th position and retrieves the next 5 characters.

2.11.2.3 RIGHT Function

The RIGHT function is a helpful formula for extracting characters from the rightmost position in a text string.

Let's look at how the RIGHT function works in Google Sheets:

The syntax for the RIGHT function is as follows:
=RIGHT(text, [num_chars])

This function is designed to fetch a specific number of characters from the right side of a text string. In the formula, "text" refers to the cell containing the text string, while "[num_chars]" indicates the number of characters you wish to extract. If you omit this parameter, it defaults to 1.

For instance, if you have the word "Goodbye" in cell A1, typing =RIGHT(A1, 3) will yield "bye." Essentially, it captures the last three characters from the right end of the text string.

2.11.3 Text Transformation
The functions below are useful for transforming text.

2.11.3.1 CONCATENATE Function

You can merge or combine two or more columns into a single one using the CONCATENATE function.

Let's delve into the CONCATENATE function in Google Sheets:

Syntax: =CONCATENATE(string1, string2,...)

This function is designed to combine multiple strings or cell values into a single string. In the syntax, "string1," "string2," and so forth represent the strings or cell references you want to concatenate.

For example:

If you have "Hello" in cell A1 and "World" in cell B1, typing =CONCATENATE(A1, " ", B1) will result in "Hello World." It concatenates the contents of cell A1, a space, and the contents of cell B1 into one string.

2.11.3.2 SPLIT Function

The SPLIT formula proves quite handy when you encounter cells with more than one combined value. By specifying a delimiter, you can split the string or text into multiple cells.

Let's explore the SPLIT function:

Syntax: =SPLIT(text, delimiter, [split_by_each], [remove_empty_text])

This function helps break down a text string into separate elements based on a specified delimiter. Here's what each part of the syntax represents:

- "text": This refers to the cell containing the text string you want to split.
- "delimiter": This is the character or characters used to separate the text into different parts.
- "[split_by_each]": This is an optional parameter that determines whether the split should be done for each character in the delimiter. It defaults to false.
- "[remove_empty_text]": Also optional, this parameter decides if empty strings should be removed from the result. It defaults to false.

For example:

If you have the text "apple,orange,banana" in cell A1, and you want to split it by commas, you would use =SPLIT(A1, ","). This function would separate "apple," "orange," and "banana" into different cells.

2.11.3.3 SUBSTITUTE Function

When you need to replace a particular word or character, the SUBSTITUTE function comes in handy. For instance, if there's a misspelled word like "gate" that should be "date," you can effortlessly correct it using the SUBSTITUTE function.

Let's dive into the SUBSTITUTE function:

Syntax: =SUBSTITUTE(text, old_text, new_text, [instance_num])

This function helps replace occurrences of a specific text within a larger text string with a new text. Here's what each part of the syntax represents:

- "text": This refers to the cell or text string where you want to perform the substitution.
- "old_text": This is the text you want to replace.
- "new_text": This is the new text that will replace the old text.
- "[instance_num]": This is an optional parameter that specifies which occurrence of the old text you want to replace. If omitted, all occurrences are replaced.

For example:

If you have the text "I love cake, cake is delicious" in cell A1, and you want to replace "cake" with "pie," you would use =SUBSTITUTE(A1, "cake", "pie"). This function would result in "I love pie, pie is delicious."

2.11.4 Meta Function

The next text function falls under the meta function category in Google Sheets.

2.11.4.1 LEN Function

This helpful formula counts the total characters in a cell. Keep in mind that symbols and spaces within the cell are also included in the character count.

Let's unravel the simplicity of the LEN function in Google Sheets:

Syntax: =LEN(text)

The LEN function stands for "length" and is used to count the number of characters in a text string. The syntax breakdown is as follows:

- "text": This is where you input the cell or text string for which you want to calculate the length.

For instance:

If you have the text "Hello, World!" in cell A1, applying =LEN(A1) would yield the result 13. This is because the function counts each character, including spaces and punctuation marks.

In summary, the LEN function provides a quick way to determine the length of a text string in terms of the number of characters it contains.

Chapter 3: Gaining Deeper Insight into Working with Your Spreadsheet

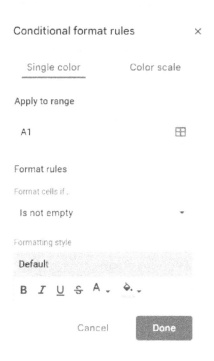

3.1 Formatting Cell(s)

Format your cells in a few easy steps:

- Launch the Google Sheets app and open your desired spreadsheet.
- Click on a cell, and then extend the selection by dragging the blue markers across neighboring cells.

- Click on "Format" in the menu.
- Navigate to the "Text" tab. Within the text tab, you have a variety of options to format your text, such as options for:

a) Adjusting text rotation

b) Modifying text size, color, and style

c) Aligning text to the bottom, middle, or top

d) Aligning text to the right, center, or left

e) Applying formatting options such as strikethrough, underline, italic, and bold

- Navigate to the "Cell" tab. Within the cell tab, you have several options to format your cell:

a) Adjust the cell fill color.

b) Apply alternating colors.

c) Add borders, including cell borders, border styles, and border colors.

d) Enable text wrapping.

e) Merge cells.

- Once you've made your desired changes, tap the sheet to save them.

3.2 Data Table

A Google Sheets table is a valuable tool for organizing and analyzing your data efficiently. Let's walk through the process of creating a Google Sheets table, step by step.

Crafting a Google Sheets data table is a straightforward process:

- Launch Google Sheets and start a new spreadsheet.
- Type in the column titles for the data table in the initial row.
- Fill in the data for every row under the appropriate columns.
- Select the data you wish to add to the table.
- Proceed to the menu bar, click the "Insert" tab, and choose "Table."
- Decide on the number of header columns and rows you'd like for the table.
- Simply click on "Insert" to generate the table with your specified settings.

After setting up the data table, you can personalize it by adjusting the cell colors, font, and other formatting choices. Additionally, you can arrange and sift through your data to simplify analysis.

3.2.1 Populating Your Table with Information

After setting up and formatting the table, the next step is to input data. Here are a few pointers for populating your table with data:

- Opt for descriptive and concise column headers, ensuring clarity on the content of each column.
- Keep the data consistently organized, simplifying the process of sorting and filtering for better accessibility.
- Implement formulas for automatic value calculations, deriving data from other cells within your table.
- Employ data validation to guarantee that the entered data aligns with specific criteria, maintaining accuracy and reliability.

3.2.2 Tips for Table Formatting

Once your table is set up, consider tweaking its format to enhance readability and analysis. Below are suggestions to help you format your table effectively:

- Highlight crucial details in your table by employing bold or italic text.

- Distinguish between the various types of data in your table by utilizing diverse font sizes or colors.
- Differentiate sections of your table by employing borders.
- Employ conditional formatting to emphasize cells that meet specific criteria.

Formatting your table in a consistent and clear manner enhances readability and comprehension while also boosting its visual appeal.

3.3 Charts and Graphs

Creating a graph or chart in Google Sheets is a straightforward process.

Once you have inputted your data into the Google Sheets spreadsheet, you might wish to visualize it for better clarity. Fortunately, Google Sheets offers a simple way to transform your data into a chart or graph. It's as simple as pie, if you catch my drift.

Google Sheets offers a range of choices for your graph. If you need to illustrate components forming a whole, a pie chart is suitable. For comparing statistics, a bar graph is likely more appropriate. Here's our guide, step by step, for creating a graph in Google Sheets.

- Choose the cells containing the data you want to use for your bar graph. Ensure that you include a column of names and corresponding values, along with a title for the values.
- Click on the "Insert" option.
- Choose "Chart" from the drop-down menu.
- Decide on the type of chart you want to create. Histograms are more suitable for comparing data over time, while pie charts are ideal when your data totals 100 percent.
- Explore the "Chart Types" option to access various choices, such as switching between columns and rows or selecting different types of graphs.
- Click on "Customization" to access more formatting choices.
- Finally, click on "Insert."

Congratulations! You've successfully inserted a graph into your spreadsheet.

3.4 Introduction to Conditional Formatting

Conditional formatting in Google Sheets allows you to automatically adjust font properties and cell background colors based on rules you establish. In simple terms, this feature enhances data visibility by visually distinguishing specific values. By coloring cells, you can emphasize key information, making complex tables easier to comprehend. With conditional formatting, your data becomes more visually appealing and easier for humans to interpret.

Conditional formatting is versatile and applicable in various workflows for visualizing data patterns, identifying issues, highlighting positive trends, and even detecting erroneous data. It stands out as one of the most widely applicable tools within Google Sheets, serving numerous purposes across different applications.

Sales managers seek rapid insights from extensive sales data, employing conditional formatting for this purpose. Accountants aim to emphasize negative values in red within their profit and loss projections, achieving this through the application of conditional formatting. Project managers seek to comprehend their resource usage effectively, and once more, conditional formatting proves invaluable for this task.

Conditional formatting isn't just about making data look good; it's also about tracking goals effectively by visually showing progress against specific metrics. In large organizations, daily and weekly reports are plentiful. Without conditional formatting, these reports can be overwhelming and lack immediate meaning. Therefore, integrating conditional formatting into your Google Sheets tables can greatly enhance their usefulness and clarity.

3.4.1 How to Apply Conditional Formatting in Google Sheets

Before delving into specifics, it's essential to grasp that working with conditional formatting adheres to a consistent pattern, comprising three crucial elements:

- Range: This refers to the cell or cells where the rule will take effect.
- Trigger: It specifies the condition that must be met for the rule to apply. For instance, the trigger could be "less than."
- Style: Once the rule is activated, it modifies the cell's appearance according to the chosen style.

Here are the steps you should take:

- Click on "Format" and then "Conditional Formatting."

- Choose the range you want to apply the formatting to.
- Set up your conditional formatting rules accordingly.
- Proceed to "Formatting Style" and choose the formatting style you prefer.
- Pick the preferred trigger from the drop-down list labeled "Format cells if..."

3.4.2 A Closer Look at How to Use Conditional Formatting

Let's delve deeper into the steps outlined above for using conditional formatting in Google Sheets.

3.4.2.1 Step One

Click on "Format" and then "Conditional Formatting." This initial step is quite simple and makes sense logically.

3.4.2.2 Step Two

The second step includes choosing the range where you want the conditional formatting to apply. You have two options for this step:

Option 1

The first option is to choose a range, be it rows, columns, or specific cells. Then, click on "Format" and select "Conditional formatting." This action will bring up a conditional formatting toolbar located at the right-hand side of the screen. If you're working with a smaller data range, this method is the way to proceed.

Option 2

The second option would be to click on "Format" and then "Conditional Formatting." Subsequently, input your desired range in the tab labeled "Apply to range." This method is particularly convenient when dealing with substantial amounts of data, minimizing the risk of errors in range selection.

When specifying a cell range, input the first and last cell, separated by a colon. For example, use A2:A21 to designate your range. If you're highlighting a single cell, simply enter the cell reference, such as A2.

If you find yourself dealing with multiple ranges, simply click on the icon beside the range field and opt for "Add another range." For instance, opt to color the A2:A21 range. This allows you to highlight as many ranges as you prefer.

3.4.2.3 Step Three

The third step includes establishing rules for conditional formatting in Google Sheets.

3.4.2.3.1 Formatting Style

Next, choose the style for your conditional formatting. While it may appear unreasonable to pass over "Format cells if..." and begin with the formatting style, setting the condition will automatically make changes to the cell style. Therefore, reversing the order seems more practical, even though the outcome remains unchanged.

Proceed to "Formatting Style" and click on "Default" to choose a style, and you'll find various default formatting style options.

If none of the default options suit your preferences, you are allowed to personalize your style by creating a custom style. This allows you to specify whether the text should be bold, italicized, underlined, or struck through. Additionally, you can click on the color selection button to choose both the cell background color and font color.

3.4.2.3.2 Under "Format cells if...," Choose the Preferred Trigger from the Drop-down Menu

Now, let's examine how the conditional aspect of formatting functions in individual cases. The trigger, labeled "Format cells if...," typically defaults to "Is not empty." However, clicking on it reveals a drop-down menu containing numerous rules that can be applied to Google Sheets conditional formatting.

Let's consider an example. Suppose we have a list of random product prices ranging from $0 to $30 in cells A2 to A21. We'll choose "Greater than" from the "Format cells if..." dropdown options and then apply the rule "Greater than $20" to the range A2 to A21, which represents the product price column.

Let's enhance the clarity and significance of the numbers by using colors. To achieve this, we'll implement two distinct rules:

- Highlight in green every value greater than 20.
- Highlight in red every value equal to or less than 20.

And don't forget to click "Done" each time you wish to apply your rules!

3.4.2.3.3 Color Scaling in Google Sheets Conditional Formatting

Another excellent feature of cell coloring is the ability to utilize a color scale, enhancing the significance and visual appeal of your data.

Google Sheets typically applies a color scale based on the range between the minimum and maximum numbers. However, you have the flexibility to customize the appearance of your scale by adjusting the maximum and minimum values.

3.4.2.3.4 Creating Your Own Rules for Conditional Formatting "Using Custom Formula Is"

Among the choices provided in the "Format cells if..." option, one particularly valuable feature is the custom formula option. This option enables you to be more adaptable with your data and expands the range of modifications you are allowed to make.

- To utilize this feature, click the drop-down menu under Format Rules, scroll down, and opt for "Custom formula is..."

Remember, every custom formula in Google Sheets begins with an equal sign (=). If you're accustomed to using OR and AND functions in your usual Google Sheets formulas, you'll be glad to know that they also function within conditional formatting.

3.4.3 Other Examples of Formatting Rules in Google Sheets

Now, let's delve deeper and explore some additional, more intricate scenarios that are commonly encountered in real-world situations.

3.4.3.1 Using the Text-Based Conditional Formatting Rule

Frequently, you might need to locate or emphasize specific words within your datasets. Google Sheets offers text-based rules, which enable cells to change based on the text you input. These rules include:

- Text starts with

- Text ends with
- Text contains
- Text does not contain
- Text is exactly

Suppose you're curious about the beef options on a menu. You can easily highlight them by selecting the entire product column and setting the rule to "Text contains," then typing "beef." This way, all beef options will be highlighted for easy identification.

Chapter 4: Managing and Organizing Your Data

4.1 Sorting and Filtering Your Google Sheets Data

You have the option to arrange your data numerically or alphabetically and apply filters to hide specific data you prefer not to display.

4.1.1 Sorting Data Numerically or Alphabetically

To arrange your data numerically or alphabetically, follow these steps:

- Open your Google Sheets spreadsheet on your computer.
- Choose the cells you want to sort.
- Make sure to freeze the first row if your spreadsheet has a header row.

- Go to the "Data" menu and select "Sort range," followed by "Advanced range sorting options."
- If the columns include headers, mark the checkbox for "Data has a header row."
- Choose the column you want to sort first and specify the sorting order.
- If you need additional sorting rules, simply click on "Add another sort column."
- Finally, click on "Sort" to apply the sorting rules.

4.1.2 Sorting Data by Color

To sort by color in Google Sheets, you can follow these steps:

- Open your Google Sheets spreadsheet on your computer.
- Choose the range of cells that you want to sort.
- Click on "Data" in the menu, then select "Create a filter."
- To access filter options, navigate to the top of the range and click on "Filter."
- Select "Sort by color" to specify the text or fill color you want to filter or sort by. Cells with the chosen color will be arranged at the top of the range. Note that you are allowed to sort by colors that have been assigned through conditional formatting, but not by alternating colors.

- To deactivate the filter, simply click on "Data" and then select "Remove filter." This action will disable the filter applied to your data.

4.1.3 Sorting a Whole Sheet
Here's how you can sort a whole sheet in Google Sheets:

- Open your Google Sheets spreadsheet on your computer.
- Locate the letter at the top of the column you intend to sort by, and right-click on the letter corresponding to the desired column.
- Choose either "Sort sheet Z to A" or "Sort sheet A to Z" from the options presented.

4.2 Using Filters and Filter Views to Filter Google Sheets Data
You can filter data in Google Sheets using filters and filter views. Here's how:

4.2.1 Filtering Your Data
Note: When you apply a filter, everyone who can access your Google Sheets spreadsheet can also view the filter. Those who can edit the spreadsheet will have the ability to modify the filter as well.

Here's how to set up a filter in Google Sheets:

- Open a Google Sheets spreadsheet on your computer.
- To create a filter, you have two options:

  a) Highlight a cell range, then proceed to the "Data" menu and select "Create

  a filter."

  b) Right-click on a cell or cells, then choose "Create a filter."

- Access filter options by navigating to the top of your selected range and clicking on the Filter List.

  a) Filter by condition: Apply predefined conditions or create custom formulas.

  b) Filter by values: Untick the checkbox beside your preferred data points to hide them; click OK to confirm.

  - - To filter by cell value, right-click on a cell, then select "Filter by cell value."

  c) Use the search box to find specific data points.

  d) Filter by color: Select fill colors or text for filtering, excluding alternating colors. Note:

Conditional formatting colors can be used for filtering.

- To remove your filter, you have two options:

  a) Click on "Data" and then select "Remove filter."

  b) Alternatively, right-click on any cell and choose "Remove filter."

After applying filters, users can find the count of displayed rows compared to the total rows at the bottom right corner of the table.

4.2.2 Creating and Saving a Filter View
Note: If your access to a spreadsheet is limited to viewing only, you can generate a temporary filter view for your personal use. It's essential to keep in mind that your filter view will not be saved.

When working on a computer, you have the ability to filter data in a way that alters the data solely within your own view of the Google Sheets spreadsheet. Notably, any adjustments made to your filter view will be saved automatically.

- To start, open your Google Sheets spreadsheet on your computer.
- Navigate to the "Data" menu, select "Filter views," and then opt for "Create a new filter view."
- Next, start sorting and filtering your data according to your preferences.
- Simply click on the "Close" button located at the upper right corner to close the filter view. It's worth noting that your filter view is automatically saved, so there's no need to worry about losing any changes you've made.

4.2.3 Removing or Replicating a Filter View

- To either remove or replicate a filter view, navigate to the top right corner and click on "Options." From there, you can choose between "Delete" or "Duplicate" based on your specific needs.

4.2.4 Removing All Filters

To clear all filters, access each filter view individually and select "Options," then choose "Delete."

Note: It's not possible to rearrange the sequence of filter views.

4.2.5 Renaming a Filter View

Renaming a filter view in Google Sheets is straightforward:

- Open your Google Sheets spreadsheet on your computer.
- Next, go to Data, click on it, and select Filter views.
- Choose the filter view you would like to rename.
- Find the filter view name in the upper-left corner of the sheet beside "Name" and click on it.
- Input the new name for the filter view, and then hit Enter on your keyboard.

4.2.6 Viewing an Existing Filter View

It's important to remember that you can only utilize one filter view in your Google Sheets at a time. Although you have the option to create multiple filter views, only one can be applied and visible at any given moment.

- Open a Google Sheets spreadsheet on your computer.
- Proceed to the "Data" menu and click on "Filter views."
- Choose a specific filter view from the options provided.

4.2.7 Saving Your Filter Configuration as a Filter View

- Open a Google Sheets spreadsheet on your computer.
- Set up the preferred filter for your data.
- Proceed to the "Data" menu and click on "Filter views."
- Finally, select "Save as filter view" to preserve your current filter settings.

4.2.8 Sending or Sharing a Filter View Link

To send or share a filter view link in Google Sheets:

- Open a Google Sheets spreadsheet on your computer.
- Apply the desired filter view to the data.
- Copy the URL from the address bar of your web browser.
- Finally, share the link to the filter view with others.

4.3 Controlling Input with Data Validation

Data validation allows you to define rules for the type of data that can be entered into specific cells in a Google Sheets spreadsheet. If someone tries to input data that doesn't meet the criteria you've set, they will either get a warning or error message, or their input will be rejected.

4.3.1 Creating a Simple Data Validation in Google Sheets

- Access your chosen Google Sheet spreadsheet and locate the cell or cells where you wish to set data validation rules. Right-click on the column's top (for instance, column "B") and choose "Data validation" from the menu. Another option is to click on the column's top, go to the menu bar, select "Data," and then choose "Data validation" from the provided drop-down menu.

- Next, proceed to the sidebar and click on "+ Add Rule."

- Now, choose the cell range to which you would like to apply the data validation rule. If you have selected the column's top, the rule will typically be applied to the entire column automatically.

- Click on "Criteria" and scroll to choose the option that matches your criteria. Imagine you have a column in your Google Sheets spreadsheet titled "Test Score." If you want to ensure that any number entered into the "Test Score" column falls between 1 and 20, select "Is between" and enter 1 and 20 as the range.

- Determine how you'd like to notify the user when they input invalid data. You have the option to either reject the input or simply display a warning.

Opting for "Show a warning" will present an alert message clarifying the problem.

4.4 Managing and Organizing Sheets and Tabs

Taking control of the spreadsheet tabs is crucial when working with Google Sheets professionally. In this section, I'll walk you through inserting new tabs, removing tabs, renaming them, and organizing them effectively. While the addition and deletion of tabs are routine tasks, giving them meaningful names and arranging them systematically is equally significant yet often overlooked.

4.4.1 Adding a New Tab

Adding a new Google Sheets tab is pretty straightforward. Just follow these straightforward steps:

- Navigate to the bottom-left of the spreadsheet, where the tab names are located, and click on the plus sign next to "Add Sheet."
- Alternatively, you can opt for another method by clicking on "Insert" in the top-toolbar menu and selecting "New sheet."

4.4.2 Renaming a Tab

Renaming a tab in Google Sheets is straightforward with these steps:

- Simply double-click on the specific tab you would like to rename. Alternatively, you can click on the little triangle located to the right of the tab name, or right-click the tab name and choose "Rename."
- Next, start typing in the new tab name.
- Finally, hit the "Enter" key on your keyboard, and you're done!

4.4.3 Deleting a Tab

Deleting a Google Sheets tab is a straightforward process. Just adhere to these simple steps:

- Right-click on the specific tab you would like to remove, or click the little triangle positioned to the left of the tab name.
- Select "Delete," and you're done.

4.4.4 Organizing Your Tabs

To organize your Google Sheets tabs, here's what you need to do:

- Click and hold on the tab you want to move, near its name.
- Drag the tab left or right to position it where you'd like.
- Let go of the mouse click to set the tab to its new location.

Chapter 5: Data Sharing and Collaboration

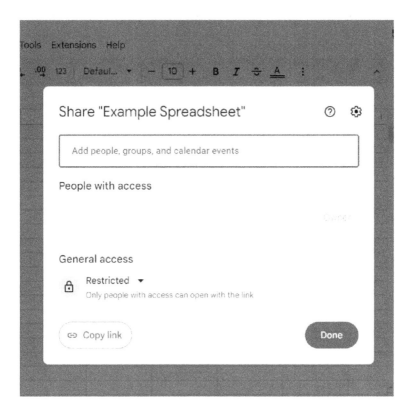

In today's digital age, data sharing and collaboration are indispensable components of modern work environments. Google Sheets, a popular cloud-based spreadsheet tool, facilitates seamless collaboration among teams, enabling them to work together in real-time from any location in the world.

Firstly, data sharing in Google Sheets allows team members to access, edit, and update spreadsheets concurrently. This real-time collaboration feature removes the demand for email exchanges and ensures that everyone is working with the latest information.

Secondly, collaboration in Google Sheets promotes transparency and efficiency within teams. With the capacity to drop comments, suggest changes, and track revisions, team members can communicate effectively and make quality decisions together. This encourages a sense of teamwork and shared responsibility, ultimately leading to better outcomes and enhanced productivity.

5.1 Sharing Your Google Sheets Spreadsheet with Certain People

Please be aware that sharing options differ based on the size of your group.

- Up to 100 People: You have the flexibility to allow up to 100 individuals with viewing, editing, or commenting permissions to collaborate simultaneously on a Google Sheets spreadsheet.
- 100 or More People: When the number of users accessing a file exceeds 100, only the owner of the spreadsheet and certain users with editing

permissions can make changes to the file. To enable more than 100 people to view your file concurrently, consider publishing it as a web page.

Here are the steps to share a file:

- Choose the file you would like to share.
- Click on the "Share" option.
- Add the Google group or email address you intend to share the file with.
- Choose whether individuals will be viewers, commenters, or editors of your file.
- If your account permits, you have the option to set a date for access to expire.
- Decide whether to notify individuals:

  a) If you wish to inform them about the shared item, tick the box next to Notify People. Each email address you provide will receive a notification.

  b) If notification is unnecessary, leave the box unchecked.

- Click on Send or Share to conclude.

5.2 Sharing a Link to Your Spreadsheet

You have the option to decide whether your file should be accessible to anyone or limited to specific individuals. If you opt to allow access to anyone with the link, your folder won't impose restrictions on who can access it.

- Choose the file you would like to share.
- Click on the "Share" or "Share" icon.
- Below "General Access," click the downward arrow.
- Determine who can have access to your file.
- Specify whether individuals will be viewers, commenters, or editors.
- Click on "Done" to complete the process.

5.3 Unsharing a Spreadsheet

If you wish to stop sharing a spreadsheet, here's what you can do:

5.3.1 Restricting Access to Your Document

Here's how you can limit access to a spreadsheet you own:

- Locate the Google Sheets file.
- Click on the file to select it.
- Then, click on "Share" and choose "Copy link."
- Click on the downward arrow next to "General access."
- Choose "Restricted" from the options.

- Click "Done" to save your changes.

5.3.2 Stop Sharing Your Google Sheets File

Here are the steps to stop sharing a document with a specific person:

- Locate the Google Sheets file.
- Select the file.
- Click on the "Share" option.
- Locate the individual you would like to stop sharing your file with.
- Next to their name, click on the downward arrow and select "Remove access."
- Confirm your action by clicking on "Save."

5.4 Commenting on a Google Sheets Spreadsheet

Here are the steps to comment on your spreadsheet:

- Open the spreadsheet on your computer.
- Highlight the specific cell where you want to leave a comment.
- In the toolbar, find and click on "Add comment."
- Enter your comment in the provided box.

- Click on "Comment" to submit it.

5.5 Chatting with Collaborators in Google Sheets

If you want to have a conversation with your collaborators directly within a spreadsheet, do the following:

- Open a Google Sheets spreadsheet on your computer.
- Look for the "Show Chat" option at the top-right corner. Note that this option is only visible when there are multiple collaborators in the file.

  Tip: If you have several collaborators in the document, you'll see a blue circle next to their avatars, indicating the number of extra collaborators. Click on the blue circle, then select "Join Chat."

- Type your message into the provided chat box.
- Once you're done, click on "Close" at the top-right corner of the chat window.

  Note: Chats in Google Sheets are visible to all file viewers and are not saved.

5.6 Publishing Your Google Sheets Documents to the Web

Once you've created a Google Sheets spreadsheet, you have the option to share your content publicly using the "Publish to the Web" feature. This tool now offers support for publishing in five additional formats. In addition to Web page format, you can now publish in OpenDocument spreadsheet (.ods), Microsoft Excel (.xlsx), PDF document (.pdf), Tab-separated values (.tsv), and Comma-separated values (.csv) formats.

When accessed in a web browser, the generated URL will initiate an automatic download of the spreadsheet in the selected format. It's important to note that spreadsheets in these added formats cannot be embedded.

- To access these options, go to a Google Sheets document.
- Click on "File," then select "Publish to the web..." from the drop-down menu.

Chapter 6: Exploring Advanced Methods for Data Analysis

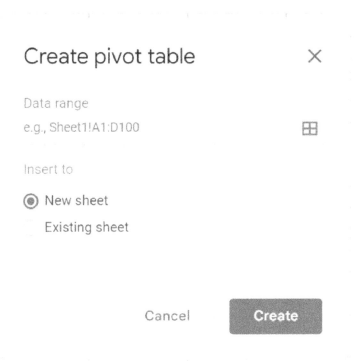

6.1 Understanding Pivot Tables in Google Sheets

Before we delve into creating pivot tables, it's essential to grasp what they are and why they're valuable.

A pivot table serves as a versatile tool for summarizing, sorting, rearranging, grouping, counting, totaling, or averaging data stored within a database. Essentially, it allows you to organize your data in various ways, facilitating the drawing of meaningful conclusions.

Just to clarify, creating a pivot table doesn't alter your data in any way. It's more about rearranging your data than adding or subtracting from it. The term "pivot" comes from the ability to rotate or pivot the data within the table, allowing you to see it from different angles.

6.1.1 Advantages of Incorporating Pivot Tables in Google Sheets

You may be questioning the need to learn another data summarizing tool if you're already familiar with various tools and functions in Google Sheets. Trying to analyze data without a pivot table is like trying to hammer a nail with a noodle. It's not the most elegant analogy, but it emphasizes the inefficiency of the process. Why spend minutes on a task that could be completed in seconds?

Here are some key qualities of pivot tables that make them highly valued among Google Sheets users:

Powerful: Pivot tables empower users to extract new insights and address critical inquiries about their data, enhancing overall decision-making capabilities.

Beautiful: Users can personalize pivot tables with custom styles, apply conditional formatting, and generate visually appealing charts and graphs, enhancing the aesthetic appeal of the data presentation.

Fast: Building customized views, applying filters, and computing new fields within pivot tables is remarkably swift.

Accurate: By automating calculations through pivot tables, users can reduce human error and sidestep mistakes that may occur when attempting manual approaches.

Flexible: Pivot tables offer versatility in shaping table layouts, creating dynamic reports and views, and updating data presentations effortlessly.

These attributes—powerful, beautiful, fast, accurate, and flexible—underscore the value and appeal of pivot tables in data analysis and decision-making processes.

6.1.2 Getting Your Data Ready for a Google Sheets Pivot Table

Before diving into creating your pivot table, it's essential to ensure that your data is correctly formatted. This step is akin to warming up before a workout; it's crucial not to overlook it to avoid potential issues down the line. While Google Sheets pivot tables offer dynamic data summarization and reorganization capabilities, they require specific data structures to function effectively. In most instances, your data should be organized as a list. Here are some key points to keep in mind:

- Ensure your columns have clear, descriptive names. While it may seem obvious, well-named columns make data management much simpler later on. Also, keep in mind that column headers should fit within a single cell.

- Avoid having blank rows in the dataset. The pivot table function relies on a clear understanding of where your data begins and where it ends. If the Google Sheets engine comes into contact with a blank row within your list, it may mistakenly identify it as the end of the data, potentially skipping any information that follows. While blank cells are acceptable, blank rows should be avoided.

- Make sure there is no additional data surrounding your data list in any cells. Keeping your dataset clean and isolated ensures accurate processing by the pivot table tool.

- Remove subtotal or grand total rows from your table. These additional rows can interfere with the pivot table's ability to correctly interpret and summarize your data.

Once your data is organized, it's time to dive into creating your first pivot table.

6.1.3 Creating a Google Sheets Pivot Table

Imagine you've gathered business data, including columns like order ID, date of order, customer name, customer ID, product, product ID, price, quantity, total price, time, and date. Now, let's create a pivot table with this data.

To set up a pivot table, follow these steps:

- Click on "Data," then select "Pivot Table."
- A dialog box will appear, prompting you to choose whether you would like to create the pivot table within an existing sheet or on a new sheet.
- If you select "New Sheet," a new tab named "Pivot Table 1" will be generated in your spreadsheet, containing a blank pivot table where you can input your data.
- To customize your pivot table, simply click "Add" next to Rows, Columns, or Values, and choose the data you want to analyze.

In our example, we opt for "Product" to be displayed in the Rows section.

- Next, we need to specify the value we're interested in. Suppose we're interested in determining the quantity sold for every product. In that case, we select "Quantity" in the Values section.
- Google Sheets then constructs the pivot table accordingly.
- To delve deeper into analysis and summarization, you can include the Columns field. For instance, to grasp each customer's typical orders and quantities, we select "customer name" in the Columns field.
- The pivot table engine provides precisely the information we seek.
- If you don't require totals, just untick the box "Show Totals."

And that wraps it up! It's straightforward and elegant. Most importantly, you acquire entirely new insights into your data.

6.1.4 Allowing Google to Generate Pivot Tables Automatically

In Google Sheets, as you're building a pivot table, the spreadsheet conveniently offers pre-made pivot table options right within the editing window.

Google can expedite the creation of a table with minimal effort on your part. You won't have to manually select rows, values, or columns, making the process faster and more efficient.

Google Sheets comes with the Explore tool, which simplifies the process of creating pivot tables. You can find this tool by locating the star-shaped button at the bottom-right corner of the Google Sheets spreadsheet. Alternatively, you can use keyboard shortcuts like Option+Shift+X for Mac or Alt+Shift+X for Windows to access it quickly.

When you click on the Explore tool, a dialog window appears, offering you two options:

- A suggested pivot table.
- More options if the suggested one doesn't suit your needs.

While the suggested pivot table can be helpful, it's beneficial to learn how to create your own. The real power of pivot tables lies in their customization options and flexibility.

6.2 Exploring Advanced Functions for Analyzing Data

Delving into data analytics involves navigating a vast terrain. It encompasses various advanced computational methods and intricate statistical models aimed at unveiling trends and patterns hidden within extensive datasets.

Fundamentally, data analytics is about deciphering data. While spreadsheets excel at organizing finances and performing calculations, they fall short of providing insights into the significance of the data they contain.

Employing functions to compare and sift through data allows you to pinpoint areas of significance and derive insights from them. For instance, while a cursory look might indicate the top-selling products in your company's lineup, only data analysis can reveal which products are experiencing growth in sales and driving higher profits.

Typically, data analysis involves dissecting the data to uncover the underlying reasons behind the numbers and assemble the broader context.

Most people are familiar with basic functions like COUNT, AVERAGE, or SUM, which serve well in many cases. Yet, for thorough data analysis, a bit more is required. Thankfully, Google Sheets offers a range of functions specifically designed for analytics tasks.

6.2.1 VLOOKUP

A significant aspect of analytics boils down to uncovering information. Handling a single sheet with a handful of entries might not pose much challenge, but when dealing with expansive projects spread across numerous spreadsheets housing hundreds of data lines, a systematic method of searching becomes imperative.

The VLOOKUP formula is designed for precisely this purpose. VLOOKUP, short for 'vertical lookup,' searches for a specified value in vertical columns. It's recommended to organize data using columns as fields to facilitate smoother VLOOKUP operations.

The challenge with the function is that it demands an exact match; if you're seeking an approximate one, then VLOOKUP isn't the right tool for the job.

The syntax for VLOOKUP consists of four essential components:

- Search Key: This is the value you want to look up in the first column of your data range. It's like telling Google Sheets, "Hey, find this for me!"
- Range: The range refers to the entire table of data where you want Google Sheets to search for your key. This includes both the column where you want to find the value and the columns where you want to pull additional data.
- Index: The index indicates which column in the specified range has the data you want to retrieve. If your table has several columns, you need to tell Google Sheets which one to look at.
- Is Sorted (Optional): This parameter is optional and lets Google Sheets know whether your data is sorted in ascending order. If it is, you can set this to TRUE for a more efficient search; otherwise, use FALSE.

Now, let's break down the syntax with a straightforward example:

Assume you have a table of products with their respective prices. You want to find the price of a specific product, such as "ProductZ." Here's how you would set up the VLOOKUP function:

=VLOOKUP("ProductZ", B2:C10, 2, FALSE)

- "ProductZ" is your search key.
- B2:C10 is your data range.
- 2 indicates the second column where the price is located.
- FALSE signifies that your data is not sorted.

This function tells Google Sheets to locate "ProductZ" in the second column of your table, then fetch the corresponding price from the third column. And there you have it—a simple yet powerful way to retrieve specific data in Google Sheets!

6.2.2 ABS

The ABS function, often overlooked, holds significance in spreadsheets. In mathematical terms, it works similarly to the modulo function. Put simply, it provides the absolute value of a number, treating both positive and negative numbers equally.

In essence, applying the ABS function to a cell range with varied numbers ensures a consistent positive outcome. It disregards the negative signs, focusing solely on the magnitude of each number. This may appear minor, but in intricate calculations involving multiple columns of data, negative values can disrupt the accuracy of the results.

Here's the breakdown of its syntax and a simple example:

ABS Function Syntax:

=ABS(value)

- Value: This is the number or cell reference for which you want to find the absolute value. Essentially, it's the input value you want to work with.

Now, let's break down the syntax with a simple example:

Suppose you have a dataset with both positive and negative numbers, and you want to find the absolute value of each number. Here's how you would use the ABS function:

=ABS(C3)

In this example,

- C3 represents the cell containing the number for which you want to find the absolute value.
- The ABS function simply returns the absolute value of the number in cell C3, regardless of whether it's positive or negative.

So, if cell C3 contains the value -5, the ABS function will return 5. Similarly, if cell C3 contains the value 8, the ABS function will return 8. It's a handy tool for working with numerical data in Google Sheets, especially when dealing with both positive and negative values.

6.2.3 MATCH and INDEX

The MATCH function proves handy when scouring for cells with an approximate (or specific) value in a spreadsheet. It provides the relative position of the desired cell within a designated range, making it particularly valuable for navigating through sorted values.

When paired with the INDEX function, MATCH truly stands out, serving as a more dynamic alternative to the VLOOKUP function.

INDEX and MATCH work hand in hand. While INDEX retrieves the value of a specified cell based on its index, MATCH helps determine the index of the desired value. Together, they enable users to search for values within an approximate range across the entire spreadsheet, similar to the functionality provided by the VLOOKUP function.

Let's take a look at how to use the MATCH and INDEX functions in Google Sheets, both of which are quite handy for data analysis tasks.

MATCH Function Syntax:

The MATCH function in Google Sheets helps you find the relative position of a specified value within a range. Here's the syntax:

=MATCH(search_key, range, [search_type])

- search_key: This is the value you want to find within the specified range.

- range: The range of cells where Google Sheets should look for the search_key.
- [search_type]: An optional parameter that defines the type of match: 1 for less than, 0 for an exact match, and -1 for greater than.

INDEX Function Syntax:

The INDEX function, on the other hand, returns the value of a cell in a specified row and column. The syntax is as follows:

=INDEX(range, row_number, [column_number])

- range: The range of cells from which to retrieve the value.
- row_number: The row number within the range from which to get the value.
- [column_number]: An optional parameter representing the column number within the range. If omitted, the function returns the entire row.

Example Usage:

Now, let's combine these functions for a practical example. Assume you have a dataset in columns A and B, where column A contains names and column B contains corresponding ages.

=MATCH("John", A:A, 0)

This MATCH function would return the position of "John" in column A.

=INDEX(B:B, MATCH("John", A:A, 0))

Here, the INDEX function uses the result from MATCH to fetch John's age from column B.

This way, MATCH and INDEX work together to efficiently retrieve information based on specific criteria within your Google Sheets dataset.

6.3 Data Visualization: Creating and Customizing Your Charts

Discover how to create visual representations that make data interpretation and storytelling easier. In this section, we'll utilize Google Sheets to generate visualizations that effectively convey the meaning behind the data.

6.3.1 How to Create a Horizontal Bar Chart

Let's start with a bar chart, a handy tool for comparing numbers. Our initial visualization will display which products generated more revenue and the distance between the highest-selling items and the lowest ones.

Imagine you have a list of products and their corresponding revenue, with the products listed in column A and the revenue in column B. The data spans from cell A1 to cell B25.

- Start by selecting cell A1, then hold down the Shift key and select cell B25. This highlights the two columns containing your data. Next, go to the top menu and choose "Insert" and then "Chart."
- Once the chart editor opens, choose "bar chart" from the available chart types. This selection will configure your data into a bar chart format.

6.3.2 How to Add a Chart Title

Now that you have created a simple chart, let us improve it to make it easier to understand.

- Begin by adjusting the chart title. Navigate to the Chart editor, choose Customize, and then select Chart and Axis titles.
- Change the title to "Top-Earning Products."
- Choose Arial as the title font and set the font size to 24. Apply bold formatting for emphasis.

6.3.3 How to Resize Your Chart

To improve chart readability, resizing is necessary.

- Click on the chart and adjust its size by dragging the bounding boxes, paying particular attention to horizontal adjustments.
- Simply click on any area at the top of the product names, then position your cursor on any side of the vertical edges until you can see the bounding boxes. Drag the bounding box as needed to ensure there's ample space for the longest name to be fully visible.
- You'll notice that there are fewer bars in the chart than the product names in your data. Google Sheets automatically organizes the names to enhance readability, skipping some to avoid overcrowding.

Hover your cursor over any bar to see a tooltip box displaying the name and value of that bar.

6.3.4 How to Improve Legibility in Your Charts

You can enhance your chart design by incorporating gridlines for better clarity. Here's a straightforward way to do it:

- Proceed to the Chart Editor, click on "Customize," and navigate to "Gridlines."
- For the Horizontal axis, set the Minor gridline count to 1 and the Major gridline count to 6.
- Return to the chart editor, navigate to "Customize," and select "Horizontal Axis."
- Then, under "Scale factor," choose 1,000,000,000.
- Next, in the "Number Format" section, select "Custom." Enter "$" as the prefix and " bn" (with a space before "bn") as the suffix, without using quotation marks.

These adjustments help format the numbers on the horizontal axis for better readability and understanding.

6.3.5 Sharing Your Interactive Data Visualization with Others

Once you're content with the precision, readability, and overall design of your chart, it's time to share it with others.

- Simply position your cursor at the chart's upper-left corner, click on the 3-dotted icon, and then choose "Publish chart," followed by "Publish."
- You'll receive an embed code after publishing, which can be used in a publication. Any updates you make will be systematically reflected in the published version.

Chapter 7: Task Automation with Scripts and Macros

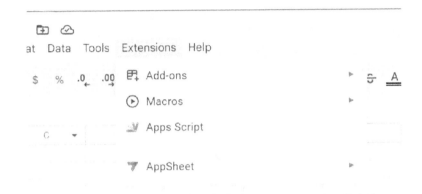

7.1 Automating Your Google Sheets Tasks with Macros

In Google Sheets, you have the option to record macros, which essentially replicate a sequence of user interface actions that you specify. After recording a macro, you can assign it to a keyboard shortcut like Ctrl+Alt+Shift+Number. This allows you to easily repeat the same set of actions elsewhere or on another dataset. Additionally, the macro can be executed through the Google Sheets Extensions > Macros menu.

When you record a Google Sheets macro, it generates an Apps Script function, which essentially duplicates the actions of the macro. This macro function is then stored in an Apps Script project associated with the sheet, usually in a file named macros.gs. If there's an existing project file with the same name, the macro function gets added to it. Google Sheets also updates the script project manifest to include the keyboard shortcut and name linked to the macro.

Given that each documented macro is completely outlined within Apps Script, you have the ability to modify them straight from inside the Apps Script editor. You can also create macros from the ground up in Apps Script or transform functions you've previously written into macros.

7.2 How to Create Macros Using Apps Script

You have the option to utilize functions that have been written in AppsScript as macro functions. A simple way to achieve this is by importing a pre-existing function from the Google Sheets editor.

Instead, you have the option to generate macros straight from the Apps Script editor by taking the following steps:

- Go to the Google Sheets interface, click on Extensions, and select Apps Script to access the script linked to the sheet in your Apps Script editor.
- Write your macro function. Remember, macro functions shouldn't have any arguments and shouldn't return any values.
- Adjust your script's manifest to establish the macro and connect it to the macro function. Give it a distinct name and a keyboard shortcut.
- Save your script project to ensure that the macro becomes accessible for use within the sheet.
- Try out the macro function within the sheet to make sure it works as you expect.

7.3 How to Edit Your Macros

To modify macros linked to a sheet, follow these steps:

- To access macros in Google Sheets, navigate to Extensions, click on Macros, and select Manage macros within the Google Sheets user interface.
- Locate the specific macro you wish to modify and click on the three-dot icon (more_vert), then select "Edit macro." This action will open the Apps Script editor, directing you to the project file where the macro function is stored.
- Modify the macro function to adjust its behavior as needed.

- Save your script project to ensure that the macro becomes accessible for use within the sheet.
- Try out the macro function within the sheet to make sure it works as you expect.

7.4 Scheduling a Macro

You have the option to schedule your macro to execute based on specific triggers such as user actions, calendar events, time intervals, or a selected date and time.

- Open a Google Sheets spreadsheet on your computer by visiting sheets.google.com.
- Next, click on "Tools" and select "Script Editor."
- Click "Edit" at the top, then choose "Current project's triggers."
- On the lower-right, click on "Add trigger" and customize your options accordingly.
- Finally, click "Save" to apply your changes.

7.5 Importing Functions to Use as Macros

If a script is already linked to a sheet, you can bring in a function from the script and designate it as a new macro. Then, assign a keyboard shortcut to it. This can be done by modifying the manifest file and adding a new element to the sheets.macros[] property.

You can also import a function as a macro directly from the Sheets user interface by following these steps:

- Navigate to the Extensions menu, then select Macros, followed by Import.
- From the list that appears, choose the function you want, and then click on the Add function.
- Click on "clear" to exit the dialog.
- Then, go to Extensions, choose Macros, and click on Manage macros.
- Find the function you imported earlier in the list. Then, assign a special keyboard shortcut to the macro. You can also adjust the macro's name here; by default, it matches the function's name.
- Press the "Update" button to save your macro settings.

7.6 The Macros Manifest Structure

In the given manifest file example, you can see a snippet that specifies the part responsible for defining Google Sheets macros. Within the "sheets" section of the manifest, you'll find details such as the macro's name, its assigned keyboard shortcut, and the function's name associated with the macro.

Keep in mind that manifests encompass various elements tied to AppScript properties. The sections under "sheets" specifically pertain to sheet features. It's important to note that this example represents only a segment of a complete manifest file and doesn't constitute a fully operational manifest on its own.

```
{
  ...
  "sheets": {
    "macros": [{
      "menuName": "QuickRowSum",
      "functionName": "calculateRowSum",
      "defaultShortcut": "Ctrl+Alt+Shift+1"
    }, {
      "menuName": "Headerfy",
      "functionName": "updateToHeaderStyle",
      "defaultShortcut": "Ctrl+Alt+Shift+2"
    }]
  }
}
```

7.7 Best Practices for Creating Macros in Apps Script

When working with macros in Apps Script, it's advisable to follow these guidelines:

- Macros work best when they're kept simple and efficient. Try to minimize the number of actions a macro performs whenever you can.

- Macros are ideal for repetitive tasks that require little to no customization. If your task involves more complex operations, it might be better to opt for a custom menu item as an alternative.
- Keep in mind that each macro's keyboard shortcut must be distinct, and a single sheet can only have up to ten macros assigned with shortcuts at once. If you have more macros, you'll need to execute them by navigating to "Extensions" and clicking on the "Macros" menu.
- If you have a macro that modifies a single cell, you can extend its effect to a cell range by selecting the entire range before running the macro. This eliminates the need to create multiple macros to perform the same action on a predetermined cell range.

7.8 Limitations of Macros

Here are some limitations to keep in mind when working with macros:

- You can't create macros within Sheets add-ons. If you try to distribute macro definitions through a Sheets add-on, users of that add-on won't be able to access or use them.
- Avoid using macros outside of bound scripts. Macros should be defined within scripts that are specifically tied to particular Google Sheets. If you

attempt to define macros in a standalone web app or script, those macro definitions will be disregarded.

- Macros are exclusive to Google Sheets and aren't available for Google Docs, Forms, or Slides.
- You can't share macro definitions through AppScript libraries.

7.9 Apps Script Automation

If you're someone who likes hands-on approaches, Google Apps Script offers a robust scripting platform. It enables you to schedule tasks, create custom functions, and automate various processes within Google Sheets.

7.9.1 Getting Started with Google Apps Script in Google Sheets

- To open the Apps Script Editor, start by opening a new sheet.
- Then, go to the Extensions menu and select Apps Script. This will open Google Apps Script in a new window.
- Navigate to the icon marked with a '+' located in the upper-left corner next to 'Files'.
- Choose 'Script' from the options presented.
- Assign a name to your script and hit the enter key to confirm.

You're now ready to start creating your personalized scripts.

Chapter 8: Helpful Hints for Boosting Productivity and Getting Things Done

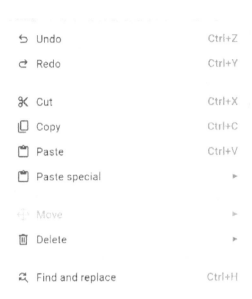

↺ Undo	Ctrl+Z
↻ Redo	Ctrl+Y
✄ Cut	Ctrl+X
▢ Copy	Ctrl+C
▢ Paste	Ctrl+V
▢ Paste special	▶
✛ Move	▶
🗑 Delete	▶
⌕ Find and replace	Ctrl+H

8.1 Useful Keyboard Shortcuts to Speed Up Your Tasks

Google Sheets, an often-used web-based spreadsheet application, presents a plethora of functions and keyboard shortcuts to enhance productivity. These shortcuts encompass tasks like selecting rows and columns, searching and replacing, undoing or redoing actions, formatting cells, copying and pasting, applying formulas, and moving around the spreadsheet. By employing these keyboard shortcuts, users can effectively manage their time and operate more smoothly within Google Sheets.

8.1.1 Keyboard Shortcuts for Common Actions

1. To select a column, use Ctrl + Space.
2. For selecting a row, press Shift + Space.
3. To select everything, either Ctrl + a or Ctrl + Shift + Space works fine.
4. To undo an action, hit Ctrl + z.
5. To redo, use Ctrl + y or Ctrl + Shift + z or simply press F4.
6. For finding text, press Ctrl + f.
7. To find and replace text, use Ctrl + h.
8. To fill a range, press Ctrl + Enter.
9. For filling down, hit Ctrl + d.
10. For filling right, use Ctrl + r.
11. To save your work, remember that every change is automatically saved in Drive, but you can manually save by pressing Ctrl + s.
12. To open a file, use Ctrl + o.
13. To print, hit Ctrl + p.
14. For copying, press Ctrl + c.
15. For cutting, use Ctrl + x.
16. To paste, press Ctrl + v.
17. To paste values only, use Ctrl + Shift + v.
18. To display common keyboard shortcuts, press Ctrl + /.
19. To insert a new sheet, simply press Shift + F11.
20. For compact controls, press Ctrl + Shift + f.
21. To toggle input tools on or off (which are accessible in spreadsheets in non-Latin languages), use Ctrl + Shift + k.
22. To select input tools, press Ctrl + Alt + Shift + k.

23. To access the tool finder (previously known as Search the menus), press Alt + /.
24. For renaming a sheet, use Alt + 1.

8.1.2 Keyboard Shortcuts for Formatting Cells

1. To make text bold, press Ctrl + b.
2. For underlining text, use Ctrl + u.
3. For italics, press Ctrl + i.
4. To apply strikethrough, press Alt + Shift + 5.
5. For center alignment, use Ctrl + Shift + e.
6. To align text to the left, press Ctrl + Shift + l.
7. To align text to the right, press Ctrl + Shift + r.
8. To add a top border, use Alt + Shift + 1.
9. For a right border, press Alt + Shift + 2.
10. To add a bottom border, use Alt + Shift + 3.
11. For a left border, press Alt + Shift + 4.
12. To remove borders altogether, press Alt + Shift + 6.
13. To apply an outer border, press Alt + Shift + 7 or Ctrl + Shift + 7.
14. To add a link, press Ctrl + k.
15. For inserting the current time, use Ctrl + Shift + ;.
16. To input the current date, press Ctrl + ;.
17. To insert both date and time, press Ctrl + Alt + Shift + ;.
18. To format a number as a decimal, use Ctrl + Shift + 1.
19. For time formatting, press Ctrl + Shift + 2.
20. To format as a date, press Ctrl + Shift + 3.
21. To convert to currency format, press Ctrl + Shift + 4.

22. For percentage formatting, use Ctrl + Shift + 5.
23. To format as an exponent, press Ctrl + Shift + 6.
24. To remove all formatting, press Ctrl + \.

8.1.3 Keyboard Shortcuts for Moving Around Your Spreadsheet

1. To navigate to the start of a row, press the Home key.
2. To move to the start of a sheet, use Ctrl + Home.
3. For reaching the end of a row, press End.
4. To go to the end of a sheet, use Ctrl + End.
5. To quickly find the active cell, press Ctrl + Backspace.
6. Navigate to the next sheet with Alt + Down Arrow
7. Proceed to the previous sheet using Alt + Up Arrow.
8. To view a list of sheets, press Alt + Shift + k.
9. To open a hyperlink, use Alt + Enter.
10. Access Explore with Ctrl + Alt + Shift + i.
11. Navigate to the side panel with Ctrl + Alt + . or Ctrl + Alt + ,.
12. To shift focus away from the spreadsheet, press Ctrl + Alt + Shift + m.
13. When you have a range of cells selected, you can move to Quicksum by using Alt + Shift + q.
14. To direct focus to a popup for images, bookmarks, and links, hold Ctrl + Alt, then press e followed by p.
15. To open the dropdown menu on a filtered cell, press Ctrl + Alt + r.

16. To access the revision history, press Ctrl + Alt + Shift + h.
17. If you want to exit the drawing editor, simply press Shift + Esc.

8.1.4 Keyboard Shortcuts for Edit Comments and Notes

1. To add or edit a note, press Shift + F2.
2. To insert or edit a comment, use Ctrl + Alt + m.
3. To open the comment discussion thread, use Ctrl + Alt + Shift + a.
4. To enter the current comment, hold Ctrl + Alt, then press e followed by c.
5. To move to the next comment, hold Ctrl + Alt, then press n followed by c.
6. To navigate to the previous comment, press and hold Ctrl + Alt, then press p followed by c.

8.1.5 Keyboard Shortcuts for Selected Comments

1. To respond to the current comment, simply press R.
2. To move to the next comment, press J.
3. For the previous comment, use K.
4. To resolve the current comment, press E.
5. To exit the current comment, press U.

8.1.6 Keyboard Shortcuts for Opening a Menu

1. Access the File menu in Google Chrome by pressing Alt + f, or Alt + Shift + f in other browsers.
2. To open the Edit menu, use Alt + e in Google Chrome, or Alt + Shift + e in other browsers.
3. For the View menu, press Alt + v in Google Chrome, or Alt + Shift + v in other browsers.
4. To open the Insert menu in Google Chrome, press Alt + i, or Alt + Shift + i in other browsers.
5. For the Format menu, use Alt + o in Google Chrome, or Alt + Shift + o in other browsers.
6. To access the Data menu, press Alt + d in Google Chrome, or Alt + Shift + d in other browsers.
7. To open the Tools menu in Google Chrome, press Alt + t, or Alt + Shift + t in other browsers.
8. To access the insert menu with cells selected, press Ctrl + Alt + Shift + = or Ctrl + Alt + =.
9. To open the delete menu with cells selected, use Ctrl + Alt + -.
10. When the spreadsheet is linked to a form, you can access the Form menu in Google Chrome by pressing Alt + m, or Alt + Shift + m in other browsers.
11. To open the Add-ons menu, use Alt + n in Google Chrome, or Alt + Shift + n in other browsers.
12. To access the Help menu in Google Chrome, press Alt + h, or Alt + Shift + h in other browsers.
13. If screen reader support is enabled, you can access the Accessibility menu by pressing Alt + a in Google Chrome, or Alt + Shift + a in other browsers.

14. To access the Sheet menu for actions like copying or deleting, press Alt + Shift + s.
15. For the Context menu, use Ctrl + Shift + \ or Shift + F10.

8.1.7 Keyboard Shortcuts for Adding or Changing Columns and Rows

1. To insert rows above, press Ctrl + Alt + Shift + = or Ctrl + Alt + = with rows selected. In Google Chrome, you can also use Alt + i, then press r, while in other browsers, use Alt + Shift + i, then press r.
2. To add rows below, use Alt + i in Google Chrome, then press w or use Alt + Shift + i, then press w in other browsers.
3. To insert columns to the left, press Ctrl + Alt + Shift + = or Ctrl + Alt + = with selected columns. You can also use Alt + i, then press c in Google Chrome, and use Alt + Shift + i, then press c while in other browsers.
4. Adding columns to the right is a snap. If you're using Google Chrome, press Alt + i, then press o. For other browsers, it's Alt + Shift + i, then press o.
5. Deleting rows is just as easy. First, select the rows you want to remove. Then, press Ctrl + Alt + - in general. In Google Chrome, it's Alt + e, then d. For other browsers, use Alt + Shift + e, then d.
6. To get rid columns, first, select the ones you want gone. Then, hit Ctrl + Alt + -. If you're on Google Chrome, press Alt + e, then press e. For other browsers, go for Alt + Shift + e, then press e.

7. Conceal a row by pressing Ctrl + Alt + 9. To reveal it again, simply use Ctrl + Shift + 9.
8. To hide a column, hit Ctrl + Alt + 0. Bring it back with Ctrl + Shift + 0.
9. To group columns or rows, press Alt + Shift + Right Arrow. Undo the grouping by hitting Alt + Shift + Left Arrow.
10. Expanding grouped columns or rows is as easy as Alt + Shift + Down Arrow. Collapse them again with Alt + Shift + Up Arrow.

8.1.8 Keyboard Shortcuts for Using Formulas

1. Display all formulas by pressing Ctrl + ~ on your keyboard.
2. Insert an array formula with the Ctrl + Shift + Enter keys on your keyboard.
3. Collapse an expanded array formula by pressing Ctrl + e.
4. To reveal or conceal formula assistance while inputting, use Shift + F1.
5. For comprehensive or concise formula assistance, press F1 during formula input.
6. Alter between absolute and relative references with F4.
7. Preview formula results by pressing F9 during formula entry.
8. Adjust the formula bar's size by moving it up or down with Ctrl + Up / Ctrl + Down.
9. Switch between formula range selection modes using F2 or Ctrl + e.

8.1.9 Keyboard Shortcuts for Screen Readers Help

1. Activate screen reader support with Ctrl + Alt + z.
2. Enable braille support by pressing Ctrl + Alt + h.
3. To have a column read aloud, use Ctrl + Alt + Shift + c.
4. For reading a row, press Ctrl + Alt + Shift + r.

Conclusion

In wrapping up our exploration of "Google Sheets for Beginners," it's clear that this book serves as an invaluable resource for individuals venturing into the world of spreadsheet management. Through its step-by-step guidance and practical examples, the book empowers readers to navigate Google Sheets with confidence and efficiency.

One of the key takeaways from the book is its emphasis on accessibility. I break down complex concepts into digestible chunks, ensuring that even those unfamiliar with spreadsheet software can grasp essential functions like data entry, formatting, and basic formulas. This approach makes learning Google Sheets less daunting and more accessible to beginners.

Additionally, "Google Sheets for Beginners" excels in its coverage of collaborative features. The book demonstrates how users can share and collaborate on sheets in real time, enhancing teamwork and productivity. By showcasing the power of collaboration tools like comments, the book equips readers with the skills needed to work effectively in a collaborative environment.

Moreover, the book doesn't just stop at the basics; it also delves into more advanced topics such as conditional formatting, data validation, and pivot tables. This comprehensive coverage ensures that readers not only grasp the fundamentals but also gain proficiency in utilizing Google Sheets for more complex tasks and analysis.

In conclusion, "Google Sheets for Beginners" stands out as a practical and user-friendly guide that demystifies spreadsheet management. Whether you're a student, professional, or someone simply looking to organize data efficiently, this book equips you with the knowledge and skills to harness the full potential of Google Sheets.

END

Thank you for reading my book.

Harold A. Stokes